CREATIVE EDUCATION

NEW YORK JETS

JULIE NELSON

Published by Creative Education
123 South Broad Street, Mankato, Minnesota 56001
Creative Education is an imprint of The Creative Company

Designed by Rita Marshall

Photos by: Allsport USA, AP/Wide World Photos, Bettmann/CORBIS,
SportsChrome

Library of Congress Cataloging-in-Publication Data

Nelson, Julie.
New York Jets / by Julie Nelson.
p. cm. — (NFL today)
Summary: Traces the history of the team from its beginnings through 1999.
ISBN 1-58341-053-8

1. New York Jets (Football team)—History—Juvenile literature. [1. New York
Jets (Football team). 2. Football—History.] I. Title. II. Series: NFL today
(Mankato, Minn.)

GV956.N43N45   2000
796.332'64'097471—dc21   99-015747

9 8 7 6 5 4 3 2

When most people think of New York City, they envision Manhattan, a small island packed with skyscrapers and what seems like a nonstop river of pedestrians, cars, and taxis filling nearly every street and sidewalk. But New York City is really a huge megalopolis that includes the five boroughs of the city and spreads out to cover parts of the states of New York, New Jersey, and Connecticut.

New Yorkers are often accused of being loud and demanding. Sometimes those labels are accurate, particularly when New Yorkers attend games featuring their two National Football League teams—the Giants of the National

Tough running back George Nock.

Despite the rainy conditions, the Titans beat Buffalo 27–3 in their first AFL game.

conference and the Jets of the American conference. For both teams, home is Giants Stadium in the Meadowlands in northern New Jersey, just a few minutes drive from Manhattan. But the two clubs—and even their fans—have always had very different personalities.

The Jets came along more than 30 years after the Giants and spent their early years in the wild and woolly American Football League. It took a while for the Jets to gain fan support, but a Super Bowl III victory and the heroics of such stars as Don Maynard and Joe Namath would eventually make them the pride of New York.

TITANS OF THE AFL

In 1960, in their first home game, the Jets attracted a crowd of less than 10,000—even after giving away 4,000 tickets. The club was called the "Titans" in those days, a synonym for Giants (New York's other football team). The Titans were part of the eight-team American Football League, formed in 1959. Harry Wismer, a former broadcaster, was the Titans' first owner.

The club's original home was the Polo Grounds, a field that had been deserted a few years earlier when the Giants baseball team left New York for San Francisco. Playing before small crowds, the Titans posted a respectable 7–7 record in 1960. The club's offense revolved around the passing of quarterback Al Dorow. The team's top receivers were Art Powell and Don Maynard, each of whom gained more than 1,000 yards on pass receptions. Dorow and Powell soon faded from the scene in New York, but Maynard be-

Multitalented halfback Curtis Martin.

came the team's first real star and eventually earned a place in the Pro Football Hall of Fame.

Opposing defensive backs could never count on Maynard running a precise pattern. His moves were often unpredictable—even for his own quarterback—as he faked and darted to get open for a pass. Once the ball got to him, though, Maynard had great hands and good speed. He tallied 88 touchdowns in his career—still a club record.

Just having Maynard on the field helped the Titans' entire offense. According to Weeb Ewbank, who coached the team after it became known as the Jets, "The key to our offense was the knowledge that the opposing teams would double-team Maynard. While they were watching him, we hit the other receivers." Maynard caught his fair share, too. His career total of 633 receptions remained an NFL record for many years.

Yet despite Maynard's efforts, the Titans were not winners on the field or at the gate. By the middle of the 1962 season, Harry Wismer was nearly broke. The AFL wanted to keep the team in New York, however, so the other owners paid the Titans' bills while league officials tried to find a buyer for the struggling franchise.

The man who came forward to lead the Titans into the modern football era was former television executive David (Sonny) Werblin. Werblin formed a syndicate to purchase the club for $1 million and get it going again. Soon after the new ownership group took over on March 15, 1963, Werblin decided to change the team's colors from a drab blue and gold to a much brighter kelly green and white. The Titans became the Jets, and the team's luck seemed to take off.

1 9 6 2

Receiver Don Maynard had another great year, catching 56 passes for 1,041 yards.

Of course, the Jets needed the right pilot to get them going, and Werblin chose Weeb Ewbank as the new head coach. Ewbank had previously coached the Baltimore Colts for nine seasons, leading them to the NFL championship in both 1958 and 1959. He was a calm leader who spoke patiently with his players rather than trying to fire them up by yelling and criticizing. "Weeb Ewbank treated us like men, and I appreciate that," recalled former Jets center John Schmitt.

1 9 6 4

Rookie of the Year Matt Snell gained a combined 1,341 yards on runs and pass receptions.

Despite the new coach and some personnel changes, the Jets finished in last place in 1963 with a 5–8–1 record. The "new" club was becoming popular with fans for the first time, however, and attendance at the Polo Grounds nearly tripled from that of previous years.

The Jets took a giant step forward when Ewbank selected Ohio State All-American fullback Matt Snell in the 1963 college draft. In his rookie year, Snell finished second in the league in carries (215) and rushing yards (948) and even caught 56 passes from quarterback Dick Wood. With Snell's strong play and the solid performance of a Jets defense led by linebacker Ed "Wahoo" McDaniel, Jets fans finally had something to cheer about. They poured into Shea Stadium— the team's new home field—in record numbers.

Confident that the Jets were going to be a financial success, Werblin decided to take a big gamble and select Alabama quarterback Joe Namath in the 1965 college draft. The day after Namath completed his college career in the Orange Bowl, Werblin offered him a three-year contract for

9

Joe Namath set a standard of excellence . . .

. . . carried on in the '80s by receiver Al Toon.

1 9 6 5

Quarterback Joe Namath passed for two touchdowns in his first pro start.

the amazing sum of $427,000. Overnight, Namath became the highest-paid athlete in any sport. Signing Namath helped bring both the Jets and the entire AFL into the "big time."

Joe Willie Namath, from a small town in Pennsylvania, rose to fame in the bright lights of Broadway. Namath was an outstanding all-around athlete. Bubba Church, a former pitcher for the Philadelphia Phillies and one of Namath's friends, recalled, "In basketball, he'd play against guys 6-feet-8 and he'd block . . . their shots. He could dunk a ball two-handed with his back to the basket."

The Jets had planned to bring Namath along slowly, but when the team lost its first two games in 1965, Coach Ewbank made him the starting quarterback. The Jets went 5–6–1 with Namath at the helm, and he was named the AFL Rookie of the Year.

Namath was a star in New York both on the field and in the city's nightclubs after games. The newspapers began calling him "Broadway Joe" because of his flashy style, and his picture was in the paper as often with a beautiful lady on his arm as with a football in his hand.

Not all fans approved of Namath's off-field antics, but they never doubted his talent. In 1966, he led the Jets to a 6–6–2 record, throwing long bombs to receivers Don Maynard and rookie George Sauer Jr. The Jets appeared to be on the verge of great things, but Namath began to have knee problems and underwent surgery.

In 1967, though, Namath was back and better than ever. "He has more mobility by far than at any time I've seen him," Ewbank proclaimed during training camp. A week later, however, Namath dropped back to pass and pain shot through his other knee. Still, in spite of the injuries, Namath became the first quarterback in pro football history to pass for more than 4,000 yards in a season.

Namath wasn't the Jets' only standout in 1967, though. Sauer caught an AFL-best 75 passes, and Maynard led the league with 1,434 receiving yards. New rushing threat Emerson Boozer gave New York a strong ground game as well, running for 10 touchdowns. These talented offensive stars, plus a solid defense anchored by end Verlon Biggs and linebacker Larry Grantham, led the Jets to their best record ever at 8–5–1.

Only four years earlier, the Jets had been the laughing-stock of the AFL. By opening day of 1968, the oddsmakers were picking them to earn a Super Bowl berth.

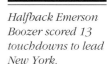

Halfback Emerson Boozer scored 13 touchdowns to lead New York.

Outstanding receiver George Sauer.

1 9 6 8

Defensive end Gerry Philbin led a terrifying Jets defense with 19 quarterback sacks.

The Jets team that opened the 1968 season at Shea Stadium was solid in all areas. Boozer and Snell provided both power and finesse in the backfield; the passing attack featuring Namath, Maynard, and Sauer was the league's best; and the defense, with Gerry Philbin on the line, Al Atkinson at linebacker, and Johnny Sample in the secondary, was tough and stingy.

The Jets easily won their first AFL Eastern Division title with an 11–3 record. They then took on the Western Division champion Oakland Raiders for the league crown. Although the lead seesawed back and forth several times, the Jets finally came out on top when Namath fired a short pass to Maynard in the end zone. Maynard held on, and the Jets won 27–23. The Jets' next stop was in Miami for Super Bowl III against the Baltimore Colts.

Super Bowl III was a turning point in professional football history. It was more than just a game between two teams—it was also a war between two leagues. The NFL's Green Bay Packers had easily defeated the AFL's best teams in the first two Super Bowls, and NFL fans called the AFL a "Mickey Mouse" league.

Baltimore was made an 18-point favorite, and some experts even predicted that the Colts would win by 30 or more. Namath, however, was never swayed by the odds. "Our team is better than any NFL team," he said boldly. "We're going to win Sunday. In fact, I guarantee it."

After two weeks of insults and hype, the game began. The Jets immediately showed that they weren't afraid of the

A Jets star for 18 seasons, kicker Pat Leahy.

Versatile running back Emerson Boozer.

Colts. On the third play of the game, Snell slammed into a Baltimore tackler so hard that the defender had to be helped off the field. A few plays later, Namath handed off to Snell for a four-yard touchdown run. It marked the first time an AFL team had ever led in a Super Bowl.

The Jets kept the Colts off-balance throughout the game. Expecting the Baltimore defense to key on Don Maynard, Ewbank had designed several new plays for George Sauer, who responded by making eight catches for 133 yards. Meanwhile, the Jets defense intercepted four passes and recovered a fumble to make Snell's touchdown and three Jim Turner field goals stand up for a 16–7 upset win.

In the jubilant Jets locker room after the game, Johnny Sample held up the game ball and proclaimed, "This belongs to the whole AFL."

After the Super Bowl win, Jets fans began to talk about a dynasty. They were certain Namath's arm could carry them to more titles. Unfortunately, his knees would not hold up over the long haul. The Jets had soared high in just a few years, but Namath's battered knees and a series of nagging injuries to Snell and Boozer quickly grounded the Jets.

Weeb Ewbank became the only coach to win both AFL and NFL championships.

A NEW ERA

By the early 1970s, most of the cast of the Jets' Super Bowl championship team had retired or been traded away. Namath continued to pose an offensive threat, and he was joined in New York for several seasons by wide receiver Jerome Barkum and flamboyant running back John Riggins.

Famed pass rusher Mark Gastineau (pages 18-19).

Tackle Joe Klecko was nearly unstoppable, making an incredible 21.5 quarterback sacks.

Even those three talented players, however, could not make the Jets winners again.

An era ended in New York in 1976, when the Jets drafted quarterback Richard Todd from the University of Alabama, Namath's alma mater. The two quarterbacks split time that first year, and then Namath was waived before the 1977 season began. "Broadway Joe" ended his 12-year career with the Jets with more than 27,000 passing yards and 170 touchdowns—both still club records.

In 1977, new head coach Walt Michaels—a former Jets linebacker—started the season with second-year quarterback Richard Todd and 14 rookies, including speedy wide receiver Wesley Walker and defensive tackle Joe Klecko. It was the beginning of a turnaround in New York. A year later, Michaels led the team to an 8–8 record, its best season of the decade, and earned NFL Coach of the Year honors.

The next season, defensive end Mark Gastineau arrived in New York and teamed up with Klecko to form the most devastating pass rushing duo in the league. Klecko was a downhome boy who went about his business with brute strength. Gastineau was a showman with speed. Together they became known as "the New York Sack Exchange." Opposing quarterbacks feared for their lives as the tandem crashed through offensive lines.

Gastineau was named All-Pro five times. His greatest notoriety, however, may have come from what is called the "Gastineau Rule." After he made a sack, Gastineau would do a dance over the fallen quarterback. "I've never choreographed it," he once explained. "It comes from total joy and excitement. When I make a sack, it's an emotional high."

The owners of the other NFL teams did not appreciate the dance much, however, and soon passed a rule to outlaw showy celebrations after a sack.

In 1981, Coach Michaels added another weapon—Freeman McNeil, an all-purpose back who would go on to become the Jets' all-time leading rusher. Behind McNeil's running, Todd's passing, and the antics of the New York Sack Exchange, New York earned its first winning record (10–5–1)—and its first playoff berth—since 1969.

The Jets faced their upstate rivals, the Buffalo Bills, in the first round of the playoffs. Several Jets turnovers put the Bills up 24–0 early, but the Jets refused to quit. Todd rallied the club back to within four points of the Bills, and the Jets began driving for the winning touchdown in the closing minute. With 11 seconds remaining, Buffalo safety Bill Simpson intercepted a Todd pass just short of the goal line to give the Bills a 31–27 victory. "If all of New York hasn't fallen in love with this team," Coach Michaels remarked after the game, "then they will in 1982."

Indeed, the Jets continued their winning ways the next season, advancing all the way to the AFC championship game against the Miami Dolphins. They would go no further, though. Playing on a muddy, rain-soaked field in the Orange Bowl, the Jets' offensive players were unable to maintain their footing, and Miami triumphed 14–0. Walt Michaels resigned after the loss and was replaced by Joe Walton.

The coaching switch was not the only major change before the 1983 season. Seeking a bigger arena and more money from ticket sales, Jets management moved the team from Shea Stadium in Queens, New York, to Giants Stadium in New Jer-

1 9 8 2

Jets quarterback Richard Todd passed for nearly 2,000 yards.

21

Game-breaking receiver Keyshawn Johnson.

sey. Many of the team's fans were irate, and some writers sarcastically renamed the club the New Jersey Jets, implying that it no longer deserved the love of New Yorkers.

Still, Jets fans found their way to New Jersey. In Giants Stadium, an additional 20,000 green-clad fans were on hand to cheer at each Jets home game. Some of the loudest cheers were for new quarterback Ken O'Brien, who led the club to the playoffs in both 1985 and 1986. The cheers soon turned to jeers, however, as the club began plummeting in the league standings near the end of the decade. After a miserable 4–12 season in 1989, Walton was fired, and a new rebuilding process began.

1 9 8 9

Erik McMillan made six interceptions, returning one 92 yards for a touchdown.

THE COSLET TO KOTITE YEARS

The signing of new head coach Bruce Coslet in 1990 brought hope to New York. Coslet was known as a no-nonsense type of coach. "We're going to be a tough, aggressive team," he declared upon arriving in New York, "and if you're not that, you won't play."

Coslet's team played hard in 1990, but injuries took their toll. All-Pro wide receiver Al Toon, noted for his leaping catches, went down several times with concussions. Sadly, the problem would eventually force him to retire. A five-game losing streak in the second half of the season ended the Jets' hopes of snapping their four-year playoff drought.

The Jets went 8–8 in 1991 and did make the playoffs as a Wild Card team, thanks in large part to the efforts of veteran placekicker Pat Leahy. In his 18th and last year in New York, Leahy recorded his 1,470th career point, the third-most in

NFL history. A 17–10 Houston win, however, ended Leahy and the Jets' playoff run.

In an attempt to add some spark to the team's offense, Coslet brought in his old quarterback from Cincinnati, Boomer Esiason, to run the Jets' offense in 1993. Esiason provided the necessary jump start, and the Jets seemed ready for their first winning season in five years before suffering another late-season collapse.

After the Jets posted another losing season in 1994 under new coach Pete Carroll, team owner Leon Hess had seen enough. "I'm 80 years old, and I want results now," he said. "I'm entitled to some enjoyment from this team, and that means winning." Hess then hired former Philadelphia Eagles head coach Rich Kotite to take the club's reins. Kotite, who

1 9 9 5

Head coach Rich Kotite arrived in New York to turn the Jets around.

Quarterback Boomer Esiason.

was born in Brooklyn, looked and sounded like a New York. He also had roots with the Jets, having served as an assistant coach under Joe Walton for seven years.

Kotite began rebuilding around veterans such as Esiason and linebacker Mo Lewis. New York fans soon discovered that the Jets could play pretty good defense, but the offense was awful. The result was a 3–13 disaster, the worst record in the league. Unfortunately, things would get worse before they got better, and the Jets sank to 1–15 in 1996.

Although the Jets won only a combined four games in 1995 and 1996, two newcomers to the organization seemed to indicate that better times were ahead. They were as different as two wide receivers could be, but together they would help lead the Jets back up the standings.

Wayne Chrebet had spent his football career as an underdog. Undrafted and overlooked in 1995, he earned a spot on the Jets' roster through tryouts and began turning heads in practice. With his intense work ethic, Chrebet quickly impressed coaches in preseason workouts. "Wayne plays every day as if somebody in authority is going to tap him on the back and say, 'It's time. Clean out your locker. Go home,'" explained Chrebet's mother Paulette.

No one in the Jets organization, however, was telling Chrebet to go home. In his first season, he set a franchise record for rookie receptions with 66. The following year, he became the first player in NFL history to catch a combined 150 passes in his first two seasons. Chrebet embraced a simple philosophy for success: "Go across the middle, get drilled, catch the ball, and get up and act like nothing happened. Show them toughness. That's what I live by."

1 9 9 6

Adrian Murrell became the first Jets back in 11 years to run for more than 1,000 yards.

Intense linebacker Mo Lewis (pages 26-27).

Vinny Testaverde had a Pro-Bowl season, passing for 3,256 yards.

In 1996, Chrebet was joined by another wide receiver, Keyshawn Johnson. Unlike Chrebet, everyone knew Johnson's name. After the two-time All-American led the University of Southern California to the Rose Bowl, Johnson was the first overall pick in the NFL draft. The differences between the two receivers were like night and day. The 5-foot-8 Chrebet was quiet and steady, and the 6-foot-3 Johnson was talkative and flashy. Together they formed a potent receiving duo, combining for more than 1,700 yards in both 1996 and 1997.

RETURN TO GLORY

In 1997, the Jets reverted to the old uniform design of the Namath era. A more substantial change came in the form of new leadership: former New England head coach Bill Parcells. The fiery Parcells was one of only two coaches in NFL history to have taken two different teams to the Super Bowl (the New York Giants and New England Patriots). New York fans hoped he could make it three teams, but in 1997 the Jets were more concerned with simply making the playoffs.

Although Parcells started his Jets coaching career impressively by guiding his team to a 41–3 drubbing of Seattle, the Jets' playoff quest came down to the final game of the year against Detroit. New York needed a win to move on to the playoffs. As the game's final minutes ticked away, however, the Jets' defense could not contain elusive Lions running back Barry Sanders. New York fell 13–10.

Still, Parcells saw hope in the future. "I told the players at the end of the 1997 season that we had to continue to improve on what we started in 1997," Parcells said. "I assured them that I would do everything possible to continue to upgrade this team. I told them that nobody could stand still. You either get better or you get worse; it's that simple."

Parcells made good on his promise, luring former Patriots running back Curtis Martin and center Kevin Mawae to New York in 1998. He also brought in quarterback Vinny Testaverde, a 12-year NFL veteran who had spent time in Tampa, Cleveland, and Baltimore.

Safety Marcus Coleman finished the season with six interceptions.

Though it took several games for Testaverde to earn the starting spot, he soon emerged as the offensive leader the Jets needed, throwing for a team-record 29 touchdowns in 1998. Chrebet and Johnson each pulled in more than 1,000 receiving yards, and the speedy Martin posted his fourth straight 1,000-yard rushing season.

With a 12–4 regular-season record, the Jets clinched their first AFC East title since 1970. They then defeated Jacksonville 34–24 in the playoffs before facing Denver in the AFC championship game. Although the Jets' defense kept the defending Super Bowl champion Broncos off the scoreboard in the first half, Denver used six New York turnovers to pull away for a 23–10 win.

In spite of the loss, what the Jets had accomplished was remarkable and unparalleled in NFL history. The team that had lost 15 games in 1996 had come within 30 minutes of making it to the Super Bowl two years later. With a few brilliant moves and a new attitude, Parcells had transformed the New York Jets into contenders.

Many football experts thought that 1999 would be the Jets' year at last. Unfortunately, the dream season quickly became

Speedy cornerback and kick returner Aaron Glenn.

Gritty receiver Wayne Chrebet.

Coach Al Groh hoped to guide the Jets back to the top of the AFC East.

a nightmare of injuries. First Chrebet broke a bone in his foot in the preseason. Then Testaverde went down with a ruptured Achilles tendon in the first game of the regular season. Although Chrebet returned several weeks later, Testaverde would miss the entire season.

Without their star quarterback, the Jets floundered, starting the season a miserable 1–6. Although disheartened, Parcells's team refused to give up. With improving backup quarterback Ray Lucas at the helm, the Jets won seven of their last nine games to barely miss the playoffs with an 8–8 record. "I think we proved to everyone that there are no quitters on our team," Lucas said.

Despite the positive end to a frustrating season, Coach Parcells decided to step down as head coach of the Jets. "I can't give [the effort] the way I know I have to to be successful 365 days a year," he explained. "I've been doing it for 15 years. I think it's time."

Several weeks later, the Jets made linebackers coach Al Groh the 14th head coach in team history. Although Keyshawn Johnson moved on to Tampa Bay in a trade for several draft picks, Groh's team is poised to take to the skies once again. With such standouts as Chrebet and Martin leading the way, the Jets may very well fly all the way to another world title.